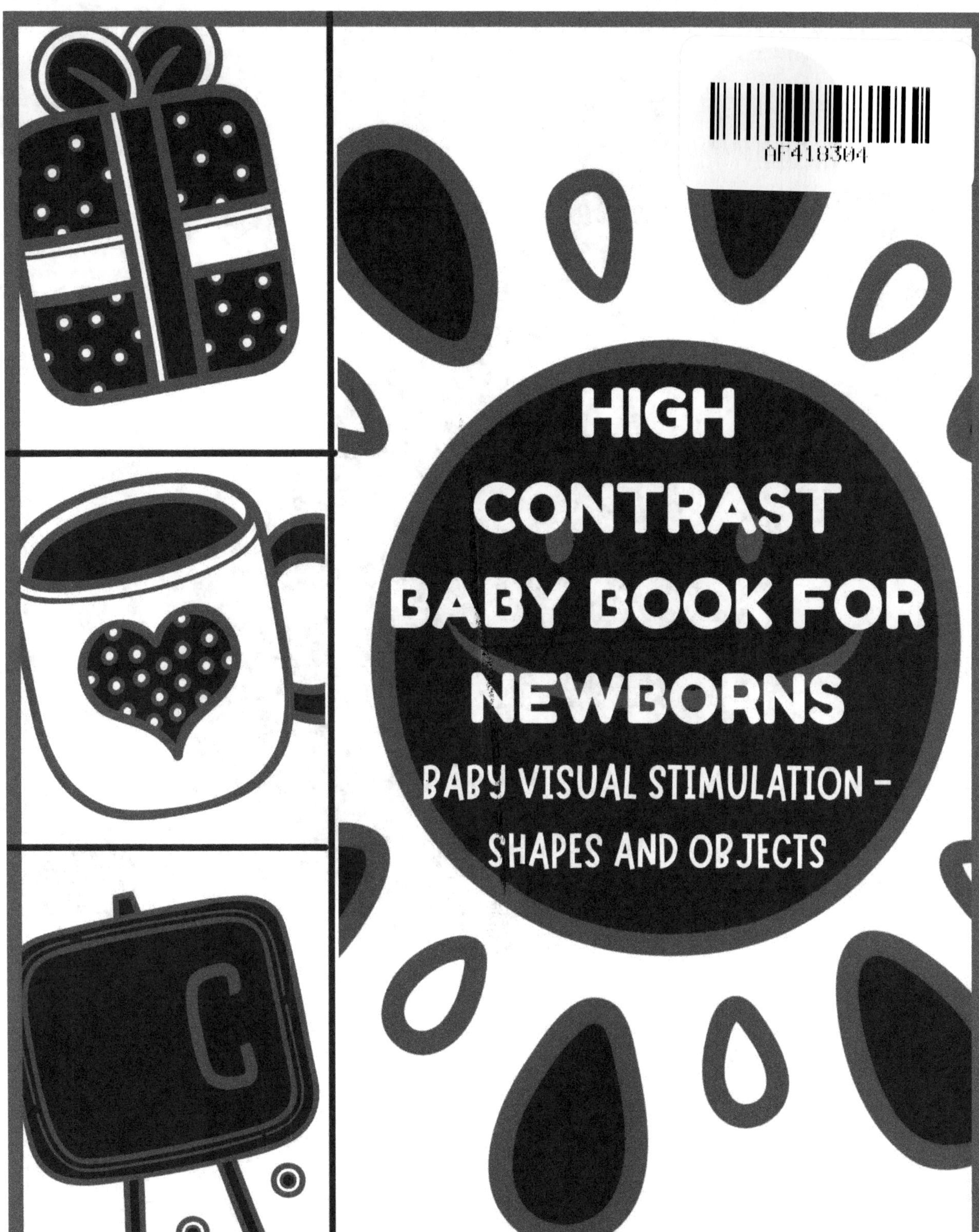

HIGH
CONTRAST
BABY BOOK FOR
NEWBORNS
BABY VISUAL STIMULATION –
SHAPES AND OBJECTS

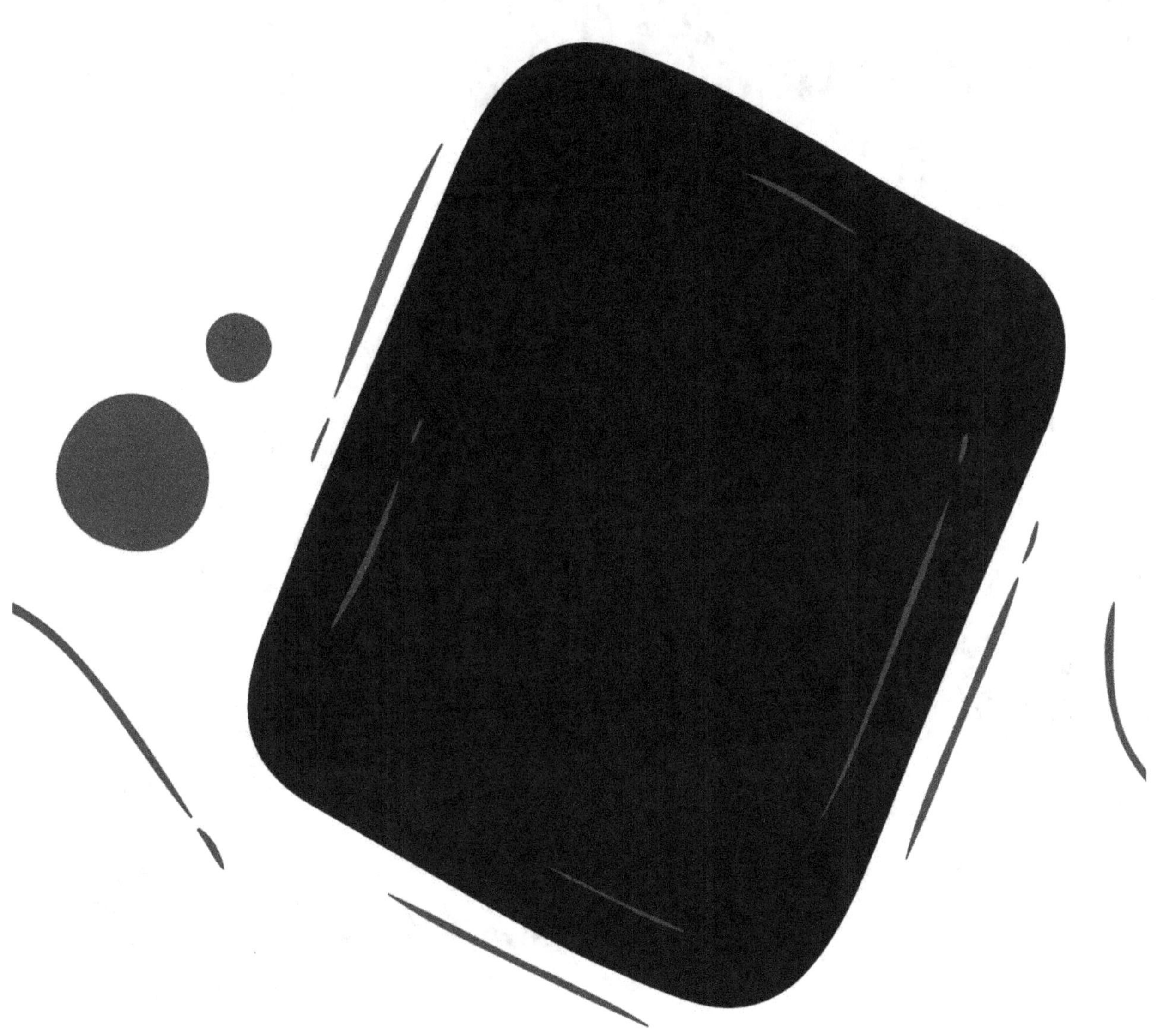

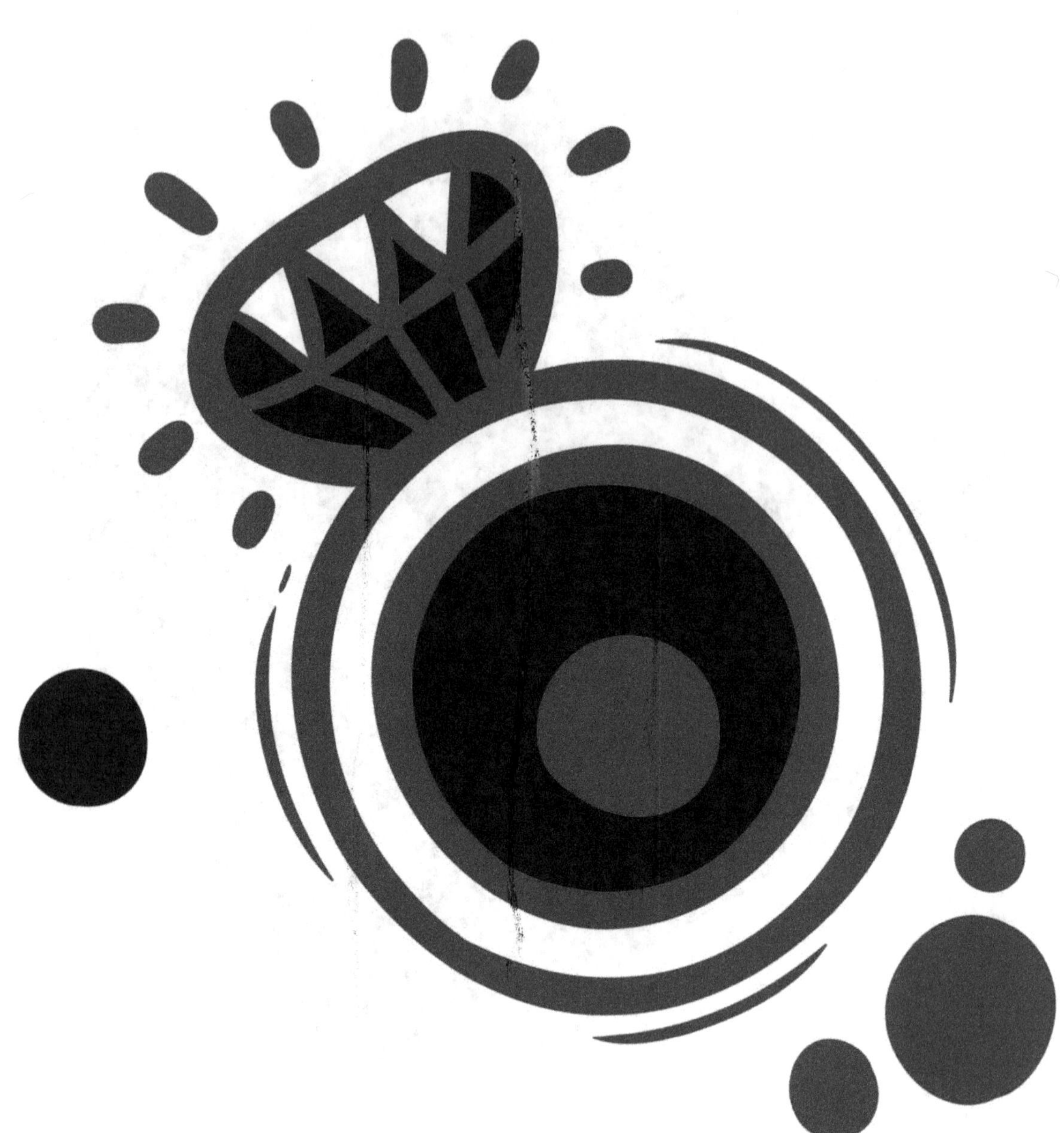

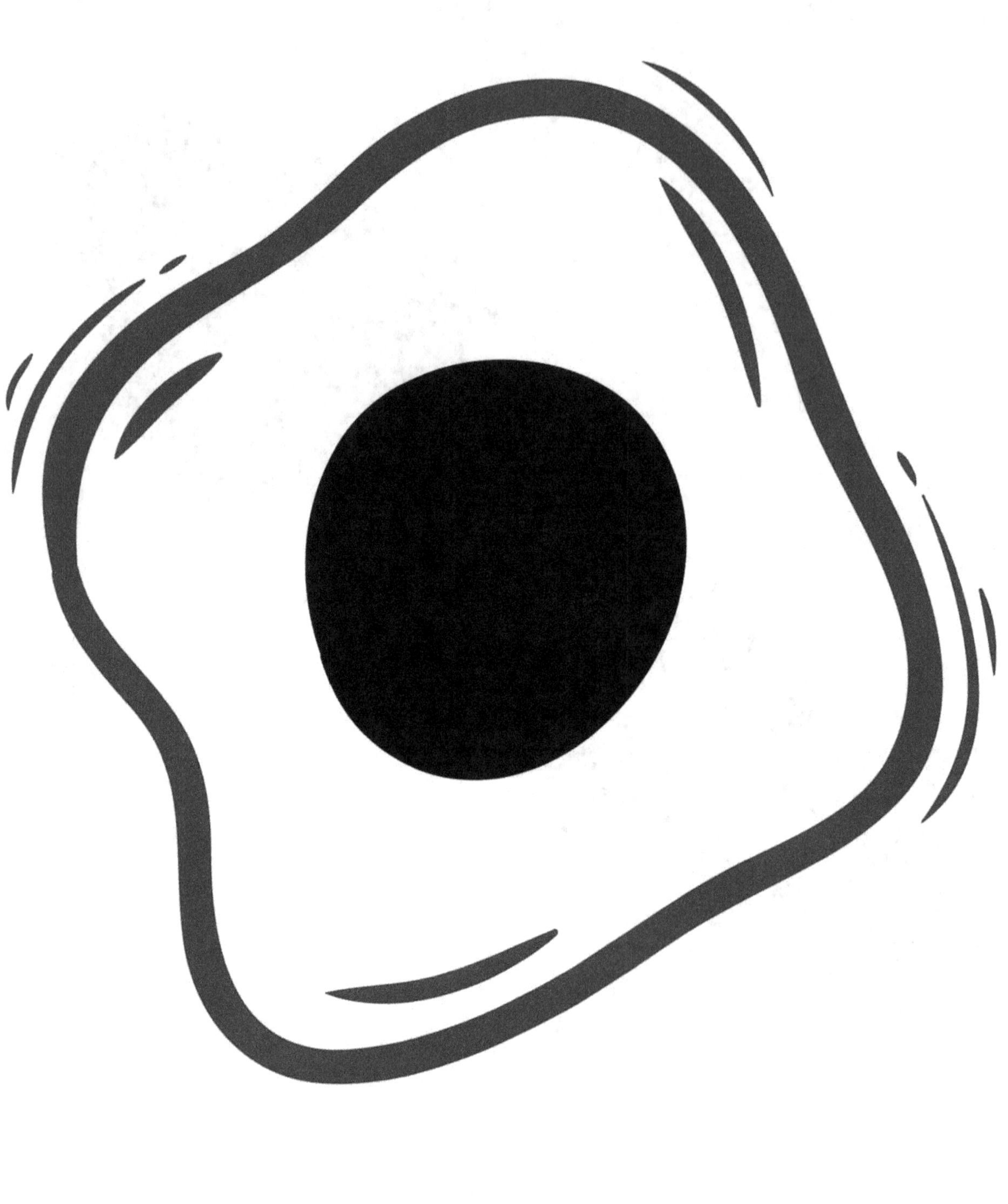

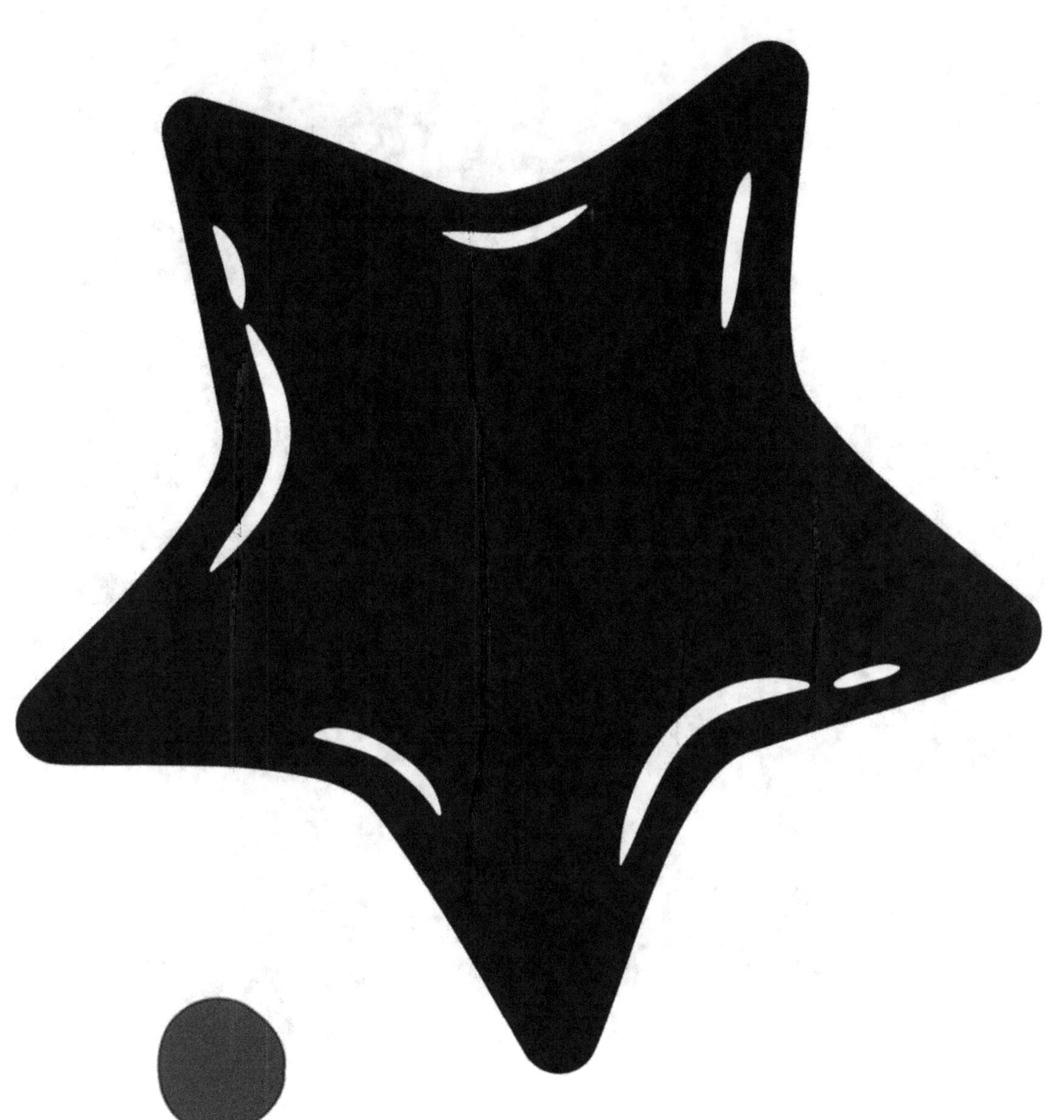

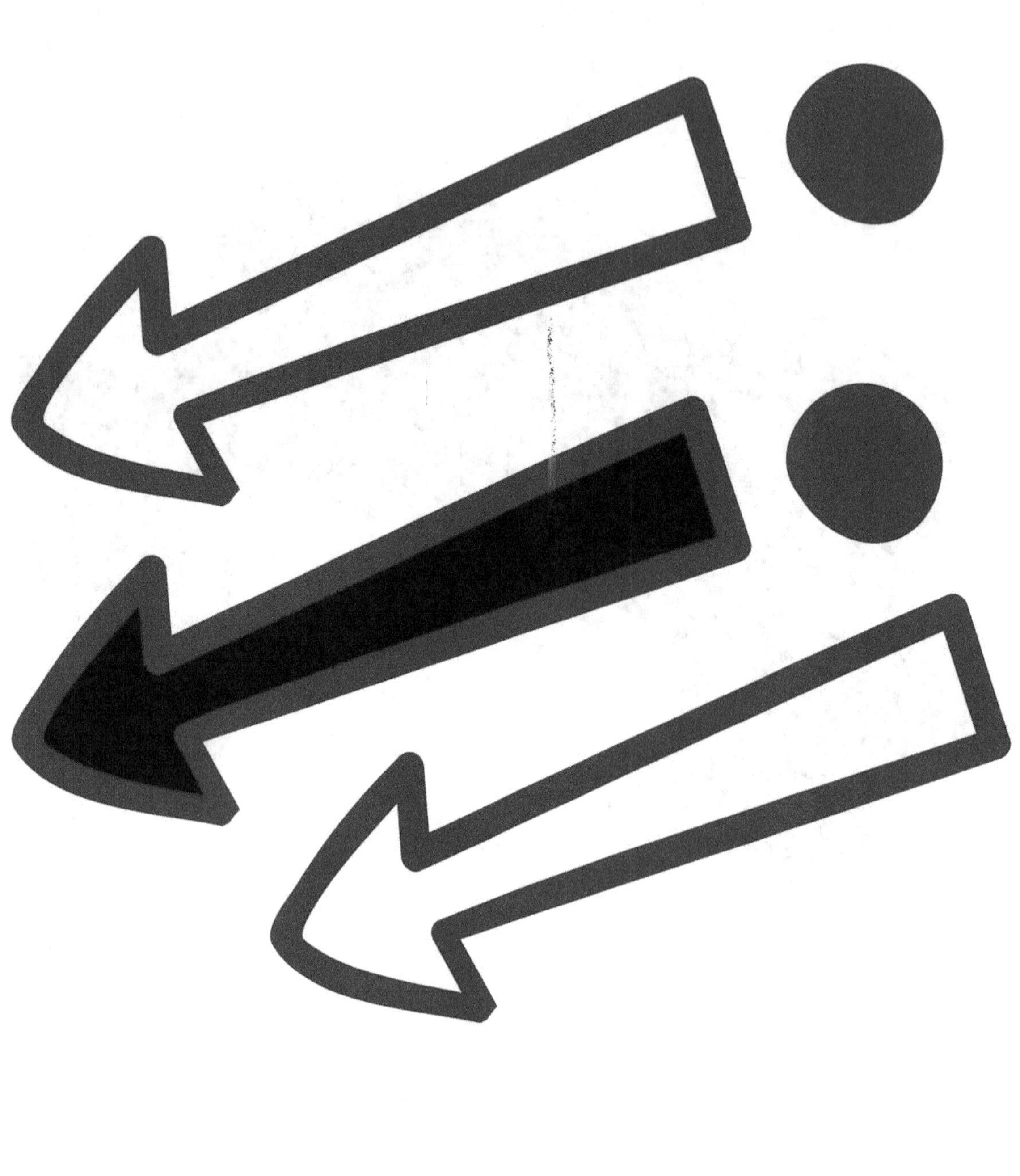

C